# A Pocket Guide to
# INTERGENERATIONAL
# LEADERSHIP

## Dr. Lawanne' S. Grant
### Foreword by Dr. Barbara McCoo Lewis

LDM
Leadership DevelopME, LLC
Publishing Services

# Dedication

This book is dedicated to leaders who are committed to including every generation at the table.

# FOREWORD

The training that Dr. Lawanne' S. Grant provided
on Intergenerational Leadership was phenomenal!
The information shared was insightful and
relevant to becoming a leader with team results.

I believe that every leader should
have an ear to hear the voice and apply
recommendations made by every generation.

Hence, I'm excited for you to
read this book as I was when I created an
exclusive forum for leaders to receive these
tips, tools, and strategies.

## Dr. Barbara McCoo Lewis

World Leader, Entrepreneur,
Ministry Mentor and Community Engager

# TABLE OF CONTENTS

# HOW WE GOT HERE...

First, let me applaud you for picking up this book. It tells me you're a leader committed to including voices from every generation on your team. This is vital, considering that at the writing of this book, there are five generations in the workforce *(Pew Research Center, 2023)*. Ignoring the importance of successfully integrating multi-generational teams is a sure plan for your organization's lack of creativity and productivity.

To avoid this pitfall, I shared a presentation with my online coaching group entitled, *Understanding the Generations You Lead.*

The goal was to share the tenants of Intergenerational Leadership and how it aids in becoming more effective when leading diverse groups. The attendees gave raving reviews and expressed their deep appreciation for the insight as it forced them to take a deeper look into their leadership approach.

I watched the replay at least five times that week because the information was just that good. I wanted it to soak in for me, the teacher, just as it had for the students.

To my surprise and extreme delight, Dr. Barbara McCoo Lewis, an iconic leader in community engagement, business affairs, and the ecclesial sector, requested the replay link. I didn't know that her review would push me toward providing more leadership development surrounding this topic and, ultimately, the publication of THIS BOOK!

As a leadership coach and strategist, I'm fortunate to provide training to diverse groups in the marketplace and ministry. The insight and strategies have proven to enhance organizational development in both settings. Although succinct, I'm confident the nuggets in this book will encourage you to embrace and practice Intergenerational Leadership.

With this, you will have more significant and sustainable outcomes among groups of varied ages.

# A WORKING DEFINITION

**Inter:** Defined as between, among, or in the midst; mutually, reciprocally, and together.

**Generational:** Defined as a group of people born and living at about the same time; approximate same age, similar ideas, problems, attitudes, etc.

**Leadership:** The process of guiding an individual or group toward an expected end.

Considering the independent definitions of the words above, it's safe to surmise that Intergenerational Leadership is the process by which a leader guides diverse groups toward a mutual goal while cultivating mutual respect among team members.

*Pennsylvania State University (2020)*
shares that:

Intergenerational Leadership has been defined as leadership that's aware of the generational differences and their potential contributions, where leaders from different generations are clearly identified and mutually respected.

# MEET THE GENERATIONS

Most books I've authored are timeless, meaning that the content is applicable now and for ages to come. Admittedly, the information shared in this book is relative but relevant. It's relative to a time of heightened discussions about the focused generations.

More details about future generations will inevitably surface and shift the dialogue. However, a working knowledge of the generations presented in this book will remain relevant to effective leadership. Why? Because it helps to know where you've been to successfully evolve to where you should be.

Let's Meet the Generations:

- **The Silent Generation** – These are individuals born between 1925 and 1945.
- **Baby Boomers:** These are individuals born between 1946 and 1964.
- **Generation X:** These are individuals born between 1965 and 1979.
- **Millennials**: These are individuals born between the years of 1980 and 1994.
- **Generation Z:** These are individuals born between 1995 and 2009.
- **Generation Alpha:** These are individuals born in or after 2010.

*NOTE: The first five generations listed will be discussed as research results are pending for the Alpha Generation. Additionally, considering the reporting source, the categorical range of years will differ slightly, so don't be alarmed. This book considers the work of Alex Atherton (2022) and the Pew Research Center (2020).*

## The Generations

Be reminded that subsequent generations will be named as time progresses.

With this, you should commit to remaining abreast of the needs, events experienced, and characteristics of every age. You'll be able to do this by asking two questions highlighted in the forthcoming section of this book.

# CONSIDERATIONS FOR EFFECTIVE INTEGRATION

Whether you're working with the Silent Generation, Baby Boomers, Generation X, Millennials, or Gen Zers, there are five things I'd like you to consider before planning for or responding to your team members:

1. Be aware of **WHO** they are.
2. Consider what they've **EXPERIENCED.**
3. Know their dominant method of **COMMUNICATION.**
4. Understand their **VIEW** of leadership.
5. Know their **EXPECTATION** of your leadership role.

If an individual is part of a generation other than yours, be assured that there are pronounced differences between the two of you. Therefore, you shouldn't expect them to think, act, or communicate in the same manner. Even if the person is in your generational group, there's a probability they may not subscribe to the blanket modus operandi for your generation.

You should ask the person to share more about who they are. Please don't allow them to only respond with what they do because often what we do, especially in a workplace, is not the sum of who we are. When you understand a person's likes, dislikes, interests, or disinterest, you have more information to lead them effectively within the group.

Your worldview is often shaped by what you know about world affairs. Similarly, what you experience in life often influences your perceptions about unfamiliar people, places, and practices.

How a person responds to you may have nothing to do with you but could be directly connected to previous experiences with someone who looks like you, whether the identifier is gender, race, religion, or leadership role.

# WHO THEY ARE &
# WHAT THEY EXPERIENCED

There are two questions that you should ask of every generation:

1. Who are they?
2. What have they experienced?

Seeking the answer to these questions will help to understand the context of a person's approach when engaging the organization and other team members. The more you know about them, the less you expect them to perform exactly like you.

## SILENT GENERATION: *Born 1925-1945*

👥 Who they are:

- Also referred to as "Traditionalist."
- Usually hardworking because they watched their parents or worked directly in factories or as farmers.
- They have willpower.
- They tend to be loyal and patient.
- They respect authority.
- Tend to be very thrifty - "Waste not, want not."
- Challenged with technology but good interpersonal skills.
- Subscribes to traditional old-time morals, safety, security, and consistency.

*Note: These are not absolute but general characteristics of the **Silent Generation.***

👥 What they've experienced:

- World War II
- Great Depression
- The Korean War
- The Cold War
- The McCarthy Hearings
- The Space Race
- The Harlem Renaissance

*Note: These national events impacted local communities during 1925-1945.*

*Several isolated events happened to different ethnic and socioeconomic groups. Hence, allowing team members to share insight about their lived or told experiences is advantageous.*

## BABY BOOMERS: *Born 1946-1964*

Who they are:

- Also referred to as the "Flower Generation."
- They tend to value relationships.
- Prefers a telephone call or letter rather than communication via technology.
- Employs technology as a "forced behavior" for productivity, not connectivity.
- Has a strong belief in the "American Dream," meaning there's emphasis on securing a job, purchasing a nice house, and retiring comfortably.

*Note: These are not absolute but general characteristics of the* **Baby Boomers Generation**.

**:busts:** What they've experienced:

- The Civil Rights Movement
- The Women's Movement
- Army-McCarthy Hearings
- First Nuclear Power Plant
- John F. Kennedy was elected President, Rosa Parks refused to move to the back of the bus, and Martin Luther King led the March on Washington.
- Dramatic shifts in opportunities as it relates to education, economics, and socialization.

*Note: These national events impacted local communities during **1946-1964**.*

*Several isolated events happened to different ethnic and socioeconomic groups. Hence, allowing team members to share insight about their lived or told experiences is advantageous.*

## GENERATION X: *Born 1965-1979*

👥 Who they are:

- Also referred to as the "Sandwich Generation."
- Has a strong conviction about Work-Life Balance.
- Most delayed marriage and childbearing to focus on their goals.
- Not afraid to confront corruption and abuse.
- Their human dignity is qualified by their freedom to do and become what they desire.

*Note: These are not absolute but general characteristics of **Generation X**.*

**👥** What they've experienced:

- The Energy Crisis
- Jonestown Mass Suicide
- Watergate Scandal
- Fall of Berlin Wall
- Operation Desert Storm
- Stock Market Decline
- Corporate Layoffs
- Terrorism at the Munich Olympics

*Note: These national events impacted local communities during **1965-1979**.*

*Several isolated events happened to different ethnic and socioeconomic groups. Hence, allowing team members to share insight about their lived or told experiences is advantageous.*

## MILLENNIALS: *Born 1980-1994*

Who they are:

- Also referred to as the "Entitled Generation."
- Has a strong skillset for technology, using it for every aspect of life engagement.
- Lacks interpersonal skills.
- Impacted by depression at higher rates.
- Motivated by innovation and start-ups.
- Chooses entrepreneurship versus traditional work environments.
- Tend to be compulsive job-hoppers.
- Buy-in often comes after they know "what's in it for me."
- Parents weren't authoritative, so they considered them to be partners.
- Negotiates with their parents instead of accepting instructions for face value.

*Note: These are not absolute but general characteristics of **Millennials**.*

👥 What they've experienced:

- The Great Recession
- 9/11 Terrorist Attack
- Heightened use of Social Media and the Internet
- The space shuttle Challenger exploded.
- Oklahoma City Bombing
- Mass shooting on school campuses (Columbine High School, Virginia Tech, etc.)
- Gulf War & Iraq War

*Note: These are national events that impacted local communities during **1980-1994**.*

*Several isolated events happened to different ethnic and socioeconomic groups. Hence, allowing team members to share insight about their lived or told experiences is advantageous.*

## GENERATION Z: *Born 1995-2009*

👪  Who they are:

- Also referred to as the "Zoomers."
- ALL they know is technology as their mode of communication and operation.
- Most feel uncertain about their future.
- Decreased value in the traditional family unit.
- Prefers to DO things versus BUYING things - *(desires travel over a new car)*.
- Likely to be less brand loyal.
- Subscribes to trendy practices for healthy eating.

*Note: These are not absolute but general characteristics of **Generation Z**.*

**👥** What they've experienced:

- The aftermath of the 9-11 Terrorist Attack
- Increase display of Gun Violence
- Great Recession
- Election of Barack Obama (first African American President)
- Social Networking
- High-performing Smart Phones
- Text & Video Messaging
- COVID-19
- Heightened Social Unrest

*Note: These national events impacted local communities during* **1995-2009.**

*Several isolated events happened to different ethnic and socioeconomic groups. Hence, allowing team members to share insight about their lived or told experiences is advantageous.*

# TIPS ON BECOMING AN INTERGENERATIONAL LEADER

*"It's hard to value IT when you don't know the worth of IT." – LSG.*

Generational conflict is usually caused by generational incongruency. The remedy to this problem is to employ the tenants of Intergenerational Leadership, aiming to infuse diverse groups with mutual respect and shared appreciation. When you don't know the context of another person's existence, you're apt to develop a misinformed storyline. The challenge with this script is that it leaves space for creating false narratives and misperceptions that breed division.

To cultivate cohesive teams with multifarious generations, consider the following:

→ **Identify and Challenge Stereotypes:**

*The Leader's Responsibility:*

- ⮑ Create a safe place that allows team members to identify personal biases.
- ⮑ Allow team members to openly share their beliefs about specific age groups, ethnicities, gender, and religion.
- ⮑ Determine why team members have particular opinions about focused groups.
- ⮑ Provide information that fosters insight and truth about the groups in discussion.

→ **Determine Communication Preferences:**

*The Leader's Responsibility:*

- ⮑ Create a forum that allows team members to share their preferred mode of communication (i.e., text message or a phone call; a printed report or digital copy).
- ⮑ Let team members share how they'd like to be addressed (i.e., by their first or last name; Ms., Mrs., or Mr.).
- ⮑ Encourage team members to employ the most effective mode of communication based on whom they're engaging. The initiator should be willing to adjust the communication style considering the recipient's preferences.

→ **Highlight Shared Experiences:**

*The Leader's Responsibility:*

- ⬧ Allow team members to share life and work experiences in a group setting.
- ⬧ Encourage team members to identify similarities in the experiences shared.
- ⬧ Ask each team member to consider another person's story, and while looking at that person, finish this sentence, "I value your experience because…."

→ **Embrace Courageous Conversation:**

*The Leader's Responsibility:*

- ⬧ Don't avoid but plan for tense moments and disagreements during group conversations.
- ⬧ Never hear the details and make assumptions without seeking clarity.
- ⬧ Encourage team members to ask questions about the information shared.
- ⬧ Questions should never attack but seek to better understand the

perspective through the lens of others.

→ **Make Room for Grace:**

*The Leader's Responsibility:*

- ➲ Warn team members that "wrong words" may be unintentionally stated while sharing individual perspectives in groups.
- ➲ Encourage team members not to become easily offended.
- ➲ Permit team members to educate others on how "wrong words" make others feel.
- ➲ Recommend how a sentence or phrase can be better stated to avoid disrespecting another group or person.

→ **Emancipatory Hope:**

*The Leader's Responsibility:*

- ➲ Remind team members that they are agents of organizational change.

- Encourage team conversations and behaviors to free others from personal bias.
- Foster liberating conversations on a frequent base.
- Identify specific actions that individuals will take to bring about equality surrounding age, race, gender, religion, etcetera.

Employing these strategies will ensure that you move toward becoming and remaining an effective Intergenerational Leader.

# WHERE DO WE GO FROM HERE...

Now that you have a working knowledge of Intergenerational Leadership, I trust that you feel empowered to build diverse teams with mutual respect. Let's be clear; this confluent transformation will not occur instantaneously. You must allow time and patience to become your partners as you intentionally bring generations together for a common goal.

My final challenge to you is to employ
**REVERSE MENTORING.**

*What is this? I'm glad you asked.*

It's the pairing of two individuals from different generations with the intent to exchange insight as it relates to their skills, worldviews, and overall approach to work and life. Each party should enter the relationship asking, "What can I offer that will help the other accomplish their goals while becoming more aware of past and present events that impact current operations?"

With this approach, the two will have dyadic roles. The mentor will become the mentee, and the mentee will become the mentor, but at no given time should the other feel inept or devalued. Reverse Mentoring allows both parties to see the contribution of what each person brings to the table.

Before you plan another project or share the next vision:

- ☑ Examine your leadership team.
- ☑ Determine the generational representation at the table.

☑ Ensure that you have a voice from each generation.

☑ Always encourage and implement ideas from every generational group.

Well, I applauded you for picking this book up, and I'm still clapping because now you've finished.

I celebrate you, and I'm even more confident that you will have a greater impact on the people and places you lead as you embrace **Intergenerational Leadership!**

## Keep Going!

# Additional Resources
## Written by Dr. Lawanne' S. Grant

---

📖 **Leadership RE-charge:** *30-day Devotion for Christian Leaders*

📖 I **AM a LEADER:** *Children's Book*

📖 **A Pocket Guide to Strategic Planning Problem Solved:** *The Leader's Guide to Identifying Symptoms, Making a Diagnosis, and Writing a Curable Plan*

📖 **Motivation ALL in One:** *52 Weeks | Just What the Doctor Ordered*

📖 **Let IT Out:** *Releasing your Dreams into the Earth*

📖 **Living on Purpose:** *Discovering and Fulfilling God's Purpose for your Life*

---

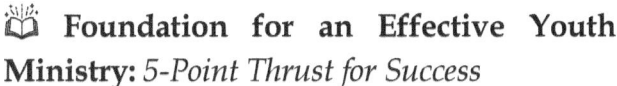 **Foundation for an Effective Youth Ministry:** *5-Point Thrust for Success*

*Also available on Amazon, Barnes & Nobles,
and everywhere books are sold.*

---

Visit the website:

# www.leadershipdevelopme.com

## *Services Offered:*

- Online & Onsite Training
- Leadership Development Groups
- Book Publications
- Resume Writing
- Individual & Group Coaching